THE SUN & MOON SIGNS LIBRARY

CANCER

22 JUNE – 22 JULY

JULIA AND DEREK PARKER

Photography by Monique le Luhandre
Illustrations by Danuta Mayer

DK

DORLING KINDERSLEY
London • New York • Stuttgart

Dedicated to Kenneth Styles

A DORLING KINDERSLEY BOOK

Editor **Tom Fraser**
Art Editor **Ursula Dawson**
Managing Editor **Krystyna Mayer**
Managing Art Editor **Derek Coombes**
Production **Antony Heller**

Computer page make-up: Patrizio Semproni.
Photography: p 10 Ronald Sheridan/Ancient Art and Architecture Library;
p 11 ©Michael Holford/British Museum; p 16 Tim Ridley.
Stylist: pp 28-29 Lucy Elworthy. Illustration: pp 60-61 Kuo Kang Chen.
Jacket illustration: Peter Lawman.
With thanks to Carolyn Lancaster and John Filbey.

First published in Great Britain in 1992 by
Dorling Kindersley Limited, London WC2E 8PS

A CIP catalogue record for this book is available
from the British Library
ISBN 0-86318-847-8

Reproduced by GRB Editrice, Verona, Italy
Printed and bound in Hong Kong by Imago

CONTENTS

INTRODUCING CANCER

CANCER, THE SIGN OF THE CRAB, IS THE FOURTH SIGN OF THE
ZODIAC. WHILE A CRAB CAN SOMETIMES BE SNAPPY,
CANCERIANS PROJECT MANY EXTREMELY POSITIVE QUALITIES
THAT MIGHT BE ASSOCIATED WITH THIS CREATURE.

Similarly to the way in which a crab's hard shell protects a soft interior, Cancer's subjects develop a hard psychological shell to protect themselves and their loved ones from the rigours of life. If you challenge or threaten a Cancerian in any way, you will at once see this self-defensive system spring into action.

Traditional groupings

As you read through this book you will come across references to the elements and the qualities, and to positive and negative, or masculine and feminine signs.

The first of these groupings, that of the elements, comprises fire, earth, air, and water signs. The second, that of the qualities, divides the Zodiac into cardinal, fixed, and mutable signs. The final grouping is made up of positive and negative, or masculine and feminine signs. Each Zodiac sign is associated with a combination of components from these groupings, all of which contribute different characteristics to it.

Cancerian characteristics

Cancer is the first sign of the water element, and therefore has a very high emotional level and is very intuitive. Possessing an excellent memory, Cancerians sometimes recall minor injuries and slights best forgotten. Yet as a sign of the cardinal quality, Cancer is outgoing towards loved ones, as well as being kind, helpful, and considerate.

The sign's ruling "planet" is the Moon. The changeability of the Moon is reflected in Cancerians: they are exceptionally prone to moodiness and sudden changes of humour. Cancer is linked with silvery blue and smoky grey colours that reflect the colours of the Moon. It is a feminine, negative sign, which inclines its subjects towards introversion.

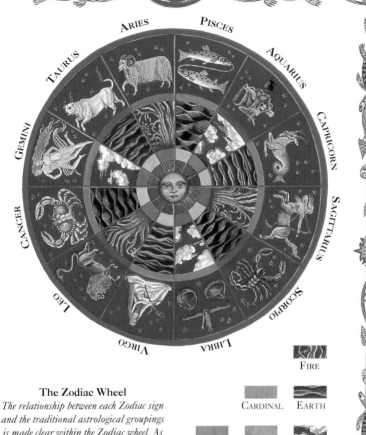

The Zodiac Wheel

The relationship between each Zodiac sign and the traditional astrological groupings is made clear within the Zodiac wheel. As you read through this book you will also discover references to polar, or opposite signs, and these, too, can be easily worked out by referring to the wheel.

FIRE

CARDINAL

EARTH

MASCULINE MUTABLE

AIR

FEMININE FIXED

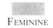

WATER

MYTHS & LEGENDS

THE ZODIAC, WHICH IS SAID TO HAVE ORIGINATED IN
BABYLON AS LONG AS 2,500 YEARS AGO, IS
A CIRCLE OF CONSTELLATIONS THROUGH WHICH THE SUN
MOVES DURING THE COURSE OF A YEAR.

The sign of Cancer probably originated in Ancient Egypt, where the constellation was first known as the sign of the Stars of the Water, and later as the Two Turtles (river turtles are found in the Nile, and have a hard shell, like that of a crab). In Ancient Babylon, the sign was known not only as Al. lul, a water-creature – "the wicked or rebellious one" – but also as bulug, the Crab or Crayfish. Much later, the Ancient Greeks named it the Tortoise.

Heracles and the hydra
In this image from 350 B.C. the crab is seen assisting the hydra.

The labours of Heracles

Of all the Zodiac signs, this constellation is perhaps the least celebrated in myth and legend. The only association that has really been made is with one of the 12 labours that the hero Heracles was made to perform by King Eurystheus, the ruler of Greece, after he had murdered his own wife and children. Having consulted the Oracle at Delphi, Heracles learned that only by showing obedience to Eurystheus could he atone for his crime. The second labour consisted of the destruction of the Lernaean hydra, a monster specially reared by the goddess Hera to fight him. It had the body of a dog, and nine snaky heads – one of which was immortal. Furthermore, its breath was so poisonous that anyone unfortunate enough to feel it fell dead instantly. From its den in a marsh near Lerna in the Peloponnese, it would embark on great orgies of destruction and killing, devastating innumerable herds and crops.

Heracles battles the hydra

Heracles forced the hydra to leave its marsh by showering the beast in flaming arrows. At first his task seemed impossible; every time he struck off one of the monster's heads, two more grew in its place. Moreover, when Heracles eventually seemed to be gaining an advantage in his battle with the hydra, Hera sent a great crab to help out, which it did by attacking the hero's foot. In the end, however, Heracles succeeded in stamping on it, disposing of it for good. Nevertheless, Hera was so grateful for the crab's attempted assistance that she set it among the stars in a constellation of its own. This is the one that we know as Cancer. Heracles went on to kill the hydra by burning off its mortal heads with a red-hot branding iron, before slicing off its immortal head.

The characteristics of a crab can often be seen in people associated with this astrological sign. Cancerians usually have a brittle protective shell, evident in an exterior gruffness; but it often conceals a caring personality.

Egyptian mummy and coffin
This ancient wooden coffin, dating from the second century A.D., is decorated with the signs of the Zodiac.

CANCER
SYMBOLISM

CERTAIN HERBS, SPICES, FLOWERS, TREES, GEMS, METALS, AND
ANIMALS HAVE LONG BEEN ASSOCIATED WITH PARTICULAR
ZODIAC SIGNS. SOME ASSOCIATIONS ARE SIMPLY FUN, WHILE
OTHERS CAN BE USEFUL, FOR INSTANCE IN MEDICINE.

Flowers

*Plants that flower at night are connected with Cancer.
Other Cancerian flowers include acanthus, honeysuckle,
and white flowers such as the white rose and lily.*

WHITE LILIES

WHITE ROSES

LAUREL

Trees
Cancer is said to have a special sympathy for all trees. This association is particularly strong with those trees that are rich in sap.

Herbs
Saxifrage, which calms the stomach, and purslane, which is good for liver ailments, are both Cancerian herbs.

SAXIFRAGE

NUTMEG

Spices
No particular spice is associated with Cancer, but coriander and nutmeg are sometimes mentioned in connection with water signs.

CORIANDER

CANCER
SYMBOLISM

Animals
*The crab is, of course, associated
with this sign; but so are all
animals with shells or tough hides,
such as the tortoise, crocodile,
and armadillo.*

TORTOISESHELL
COMB

TORTOISESHELL BOX

FAN WITH
MOTHER-OF-PEARL
STICKS

CRAB

Gems
The Cancerian gem is the pearl – its lustre is closely associated with the Moon, which rules Cancer.

PEARL
NECKLACE

LOCKET DECORATED
WITH PEARLS

Metal
Silver is the Cancerian metal. Those born under this sign often like to wear silver jewellery.

SILVER FILIGREE SPOONS

ANTIQUE SILVER PICTURE FRAME

CANCER
PROFILE

THE APPEARANCE OF TYPICAL CANCERIANS OFTEN REFLECTS
THEIR HOARDING INSTINCTS. FAVOURITE OLD JACKETS,
OR SOME REFERENCE TO THE PAST, ARE USUALLY IN EVIDENCE.
CARELESSNESS CAN SOMETIMES SPOIL THEIR IMAGE.

Many Cancerians fail to stand as straight as they should. They are often a little round-shouldered, which can make them look rather worried or even apprehensive.

The body

Cancerians are generally good cooks. You may therefore tend towards being a little overweight if you are not careful about what you eat. Unless you are really keen on taking exercise you could be a little more prone to becoming flabby than many other Zodiac types.

You are very likely to have a strong constitution, and will probably possess excellent powers of resistance to illness. A great many women of this sign have more than ample bosoms,

The Cancerian face
Long red hair, and a rather pale complexion, are both very common Cancerian characteristics.

which can be a wonderful asset to their powers of attraction.

The face

Cancerians often have rather long hair, which can become a little untidy if it does not receive the appropriate amount of care. Red hair is very common among Cancerians. Your forehead is likely to be rather pale and pronounced, perhaps with frown lines between the eyes. The eyes themselves are usually on the small side; some Cancerians may have rather beady little eyes. Even among races with dark skin colouring, Cancerians tend to have pale skins that are rather sensitive to the sun. It is possible that scar tissue will show on your skin long

The Cancerian stance

Many Cancerians tend to hunch themselves up when they stand; this can make them look rather apprehensive.

after a wound has healed. As a Cancerian, your mouth is likely to be soft and flexible.

Style

The Cancerian style is often very distinctive. A particularly smart image is often spoiled by choosing the wrong accessories or by sheer carelessness: you may for example sometimes leave a shoulder-strap showing, or wear an untidily knotted tie. Because of this tendency you need to take great care over the way you decide to dress – more, in fact, than members of any other sign. You could have a preference for antique clothes, which can be very attractive.

You are likely to have a very good sense of colour. Soft shades of blue or grey often complement the Cancerian personality. Many Cancerians also choose textures skilfully.

In general

Your overall appearance may be marked by a tendency to stoop, and perhaps glance furtively around you to make sure that you are not about to

be challenged. As a Cancerian, you are probably also likely to pay an unusual amount of attention to the weather. In your efforts to pre-empt and cater for every type of weather condition you may sometimes go so far as to appear exaggeratedly swathed in thick, heavy layers of warm clothes and long scarves when it is cold, but also to dress extremely lightly when it is hot.

PERSONALITY

KINDNESS AND SENSITIVITY ARE DOMINANT FEATURES OF THE
CANCERIAN PERSONALITY. WHILE THEY THEMSELVES
ARE EASILY HURT, CANCERIANS ARE OFTEN UNAWARE THAT THEY
CAN BE HARSH IN THEIR RESPONSES TO OTHERS.

The first time that someone meets you, it may be easy for them to get the wrong impression. This is because you can tend to act a little defensively towards people who you do not know; you develop something of a hard shell in order to protect yourself. Underneath this, however, you probably feel rather vulnerable.

If others are tactful towards you, and take their time in getting to know you, it should not be too difficult for them to break through your defences. When this happens, your deeply caring and understanding nature will shine through. Those who succeed in gaining your friendship will discover that you have the capacity to be a really good friend.

At work

You have a marvellously fertile imagination, and should aim to use it positively and creatively under all circumstances. This applies to the way you approach your work. Only then will you be able to express your potential in the best possible way.

Your attitudes

You are probably the most tenacious of all Zodiac types, and you hang on tightly to your friends and loved ones. While you are tremendously faithful, and want to do as much as possible for your family, it can be extremely difficult for you to accept the fact that your children will want to leave home and build their own lives once they grow up.

The overall picture

One of the most common character traits shared by all Cancerians, which is linked to your tenacity, is a strong tendency to hoard. You will hardly ever throw anything away – so much so that you and your home will inevitably become surrounded by clutter. If, however, you decide to

The Moon rules Cancer
*The Moon, represented here by the goddess Diana, is usually
shown as feminine. It encourages Cancerians to act instinctively,
and influences the emotions and the digestive system.*

take a serious interest either in antiques or in collecting articles that you find fascinating, this tendency will be put to good use.

By remodelling your Cancerian hoarding instinct into a love of collecting things, you will be able to avoid having much of your space consumed by ugly heaps of old newspapers, battered pots and pans, and any old junk – for example pieces of string that are too short to be of any possible use to anyone.

Having said this many Cancerians do have marvellous taste and, when this is fully developed, it really shows in every aspect of their lives. You are more than likely to have a great appreciation of, and sensitivity to, everything that is beautiful.

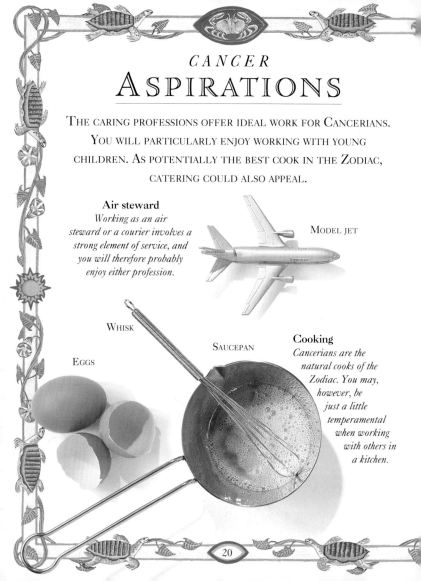

CANCER
ASPIRATIONS

THE CARING PROFESSIONS OFFER IDEAL WORK FOR CANCERIANS.
YOU WILL PARTICULARLY ENJOY WORKING WITH YOUNG
CHILDREN. AS POTENTIALLY THE BEST COOK IN THE ZODIAC,
CATERING COULD ALSO APPEAL.

Air steward
*Working as an air
steward or a courier involves a
strong element of service, and
you will therefore probably
enjoy either profession.*

MODEL JET

WHISK

SAUCEPAN

EGGS

Cooking
*Cancerians are the
natural cooks of the
Zodiac. You may,
however, be
just a little
temperamental
when working
with others in
a kitchen.*

QUILL PEN

Author
Many Cancerians are inspired by history and romance. You could be successful as a fiction writer in either of these areas.

1920s GLASS INKWELL

Caring professions
Caring for children may come naturally to you. You could find working in the social services particularly rewarding.

MERCURY THERMOMETER

BLOTTING PAPER

Teaching
You could well receive pleasure from inspiring young children and helping them to develop their minds. Your powerful imagination will be a great asset to you in this profession.

ABACUS

CANCER
HEALTH

THE PREVAILING ATMOSPHERE WILL HAVE A PHYSICAL, AS
WELL AS AN EMOTIONAL, EFFECT ON A SENSITIVE
CANCERIAN. YOUR RESPONSES TO THIS ATMOSPHERE ARE
LIKELY TO BE HIGHLY INDIVIDUAL.

Many Cancerians have somewhat pale complexions, irrespective of their race and colour. But this is not a clue to how healthy or unhealthy they may be. In fact, you have a fairly strong constitution.

Your diet
As long as you beware of consuming too much cholesterol, you will benefit from a diet that includes a lot of dairy products. You may need to supplement your diet with Calcium Fluoride (Calc. Fluor.). This is considered to be important for the health of the teeth, fingernails, and bones.

Of all the 12 Zodiac signs, Cancerians are particularly prone to worrying. When you become upset, you may find yourself suffering from digestive problems.

Taking care
The traditional Cancerian body area is the breasts. Although this sign has no connection at all with breast cancer, it is sensible for all women to perform regular self-examinations. The sensitive Cancerian skin is a problem area. Protect yourself against the strong rays of the sun, as you are prone to sunburn.

Gallia melon
Fruit and vegetables with a high water content, such as melons and pumpkins, are among the foods associated with Cancer.

Astrology and the body

For many centuries it was impossible to practice medicine without a knowledge of astrology. In European universities, medical training included information on how planetary positions would affect the administration of medicines, the bleeding of patients, and the right time to pick herbs and make potions. Each Zodiac sign rules a particular part of the body, and textbooks always included a drawing that illustrated the point.

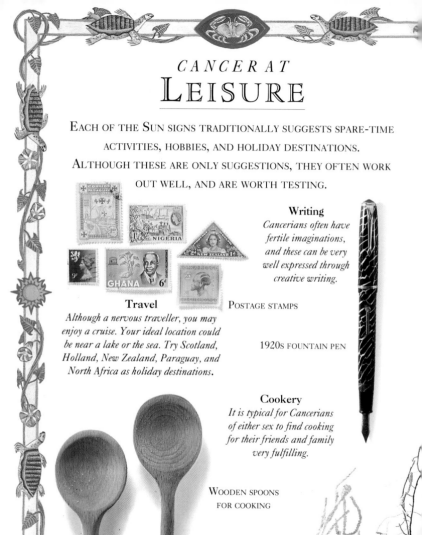

CANCER AT
LEISURE

EACH OF THE SUN SIGNS TRADITIONALLY SUGGESTS SPARE-TIME
ACTIVITIES, HOBBIES, AND HOLIDAY DESTINATIONS.
ALTHOUGH THESE ARE ONLY SUGGESTIONS, THEY OFTEN WORK
OUT WELL, AND ARE WORTH TESTING.

Writing
*Cancerians often have
fertile imaginations,
and these can be very
well expressed through
creative writing.*

POSTAGE STAMPS

1920S FOUNTAIN PEN

Travel
*Although a nervous traveller, you may
enjoy a cruise. Your ideal location could
be near a lake or the sea. Try Scotland,
Holland, New Zealand, Paraguay, and
North Africa as holiday destinations.*

Cookery
*It is typical for Cancerians
of either sex to find cooking
for their friends and family
very fulfilling.*

WOODEN SPOONS
FOR COOKING

SAILOR'S SHACKLE
FOR SECURING ROPE

SILVER
SCENT
BOTTLE

Sailing

Since Cancer is a water sign, many of its subjects are never happier than when enjoying themselves in boats. Some become skilful sailors.

Silverwork

Silver can be quite important for Cancerians, to the extent that they often enjoy silverwork. It is the metal associated with the Moon, which rules Cancer.

Sewing

This is often a Cancerian hobby. Making children's clothes can be a particular speciality.

TOY SEWING MACHINE

COLLECTION OF
SHELLS AND CORAL

Collecting

Cancerians are the hoarders of the Zodiac. If, however, this tendency can be used to form an unusual collection of some kind, it can be most rewarding.

CANCER IN
LOVE

MANY OF THE BEST CANCERIAN QUALITIES SPRING INTO ACTION
WHEN CANCER FALLS IN LOVE. WHILE YOU ARE ROMANTIC AND
PASSIONATE, YOUR REACTIONS TO BOTH THE GOOD AND BAD
THINGS IN A RELATIONSHIP CAN BE A LITTLE EXTREME.

While Cancerian emotions find a wonderfully positive outlet when you fall in love, it is also very easy for you to express certain traits that can have a negative effect on a relationship. If, however, you are conscious of the fact that you can create a less easy atmosphere for your partners than you might imagine, you will be able to correct yourself before anything goes drastically wrong.

You have a very powerful motivation to love, cherish, and protect your loved ones. Unless you are careful, you may end up taking this tenderness too far, and create a rather claustrophobic atmosphere within your relationship. Many people are unable to cope with this, finding it too confining, so this tendency to limit independence or freedom of expression may sometimes come between you and your lovers.

As a lover
You are likely to take your love life very seriously and, while this does not mean that you do not enjoy – indeed revel in – love and sex, it does mean that due to a strong home-making and family raising instinct, you may tend to look upon all relationships with this in view. You

the sign will be warmly affectionate as well as passionate, but can be very possessive. Others have a wonderfully flirtatious streak, which lightens their Cancerian intensity in love; a further group has a lot of style and elegance, and will put partners on a pedestal. Some Cancerians display a sense of modesty that intrigues prospective partners.

should be aware that many prospective partners may not be so interested in a serious commitment. You are, no doubt, a wonderful lover, since you are both sensuous and in possession of a great instinct for the kind of things that are likely to make your partners happy.

Types of Cancerian lover
When Cancerians are young, it is as well for them to learn to play the field. This way, they will gain experience of the opposite sex and, once committed, they are experienced and mature enough to cope with a stable, long-term relationship. The influence of other planets will produce some subtle differences from one Cancerian to the next. Some of the more clinging members of

CANCER AT
HOME

A CANCERIAN'S DWELLING PLACE IS, ABOVE ALL, A HOME. THE
LOOK OF THE ROOMS USUALLY TAKES SECOND PLACE TO
CONVENIENCE, WHICH IS OFTEN THAT OF THE CHILDREN. THIS
CAN LEAD TO SUPREME UNTIDINESS.

When choosing a place to live you would do well to remember that most Cancerians need a degree of peace and tranquility, perhaps in the form of a beautiful view, close at hand. This does not mean that you will feel unhappy living anywhere other than the heart of the country; a tiny balcony, or a corner filled with flowers, will provide you with a quiet, calming focus. The Cancerian home will ideally be quite close to a water source such as a slow-moving river, the sea, or a lake.

Wicker sewing basket
A sewing basket, knitting, or toys may be scattered around your home.

Furniture

Cancerians love the past, and hate to throw anything away. You are likely to choose either very traditional designs or, if you can afford it, quality antique furniture. You may become so fond of articles such as favourite armchairs that you will cling to them until they eventually begin to fall to pieces.

With well-developed Cancerian taste you may, however, choose quite beautiful, extremely comfortable furniture. Since your home is likely to be so important to you, the overall effect and atmosphere may be a joy to experience.

Soft furnishings

Cancerians look to the past when deciding on curtains and drapes. Your choice may veer either towards heavy silk brocades in pale silvery grey, or pastel colours, or alternatively

Jug and fabric
These objects reflect the Cancerian colours and metal.

Victorian chintz. When choosing new curtains, make sure that they are not too heavy, and try not to create a claustrophobic atmosphere. A Cancerian will have no desire to be overlooked by neighbours, but if you happen to live near the sea or a river, you will certainly want to see it clearly. If this is the case, curtains will definitely take a back seat.

Many Cancerians enjoy creating their own cushions, perhaps using petit point or some other form of decorative needlework.

Decorative objects

The tendency to hoard can ruin the effect of the Cancerian home. It may become extremely cluttered. If, however, your tendency to hoard can

be controlled, and expressed through showing off an interesting personal collection of some kind, this will obviously enhance the overall appearance of your home.

You may choose to display a painting of your children, or perhaps a seascape. If you are fortunate enough to own some silver, or perhaps family heirlooms, these are likely to be prominently displayed. Cancerians should accept the fact that sentimentality about old things can be rather counter-productive.

Armchair and doll
A comfortable, well-worn armchair may be a much-loved item in your home.

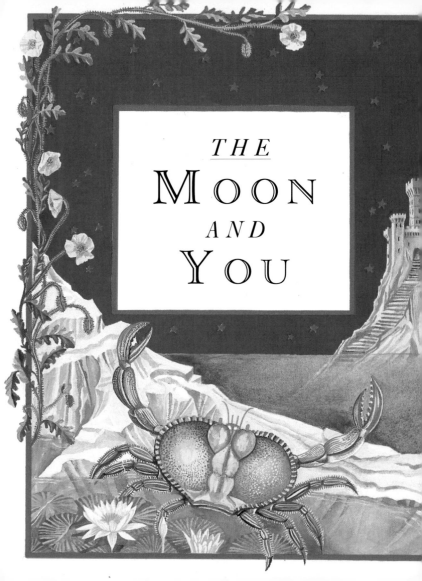

THE
MOON
AND
YOU

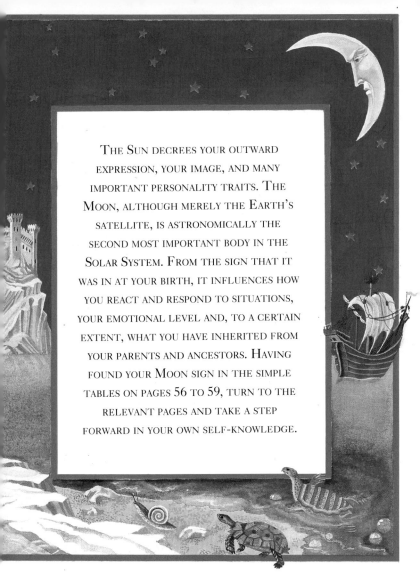

THE SUN DECREES YOUR OUTWARD
EXPRESSION, YOUR IMAGE, AND MANY
IMPORTANT PERSONALITY TRAITS. THE
MOON, ALTHOUGH MERELY THE EARTH'S
SATELLITE, IS ASTRONOMICALLY THE
SECOND MOST IMPORTANT BODY IN THE
SOLAR SYSTEM. FROM THE SIGN THAT IT
WAS IN AT YOUR BIRTH, IT INFLUENCES HOW
YOU REACT AND RESPOND TO SITUATIONS,
YOUR EMOTIONAL LEVEL AND, TO A CERTAIN
EXTENT, WHAT YOU HAVE INHERITED FROM
YOUR PARENTS AND ANCESTORS. HAVING
FOUND YOUR MOON SIGN IN THE SIMPLE
TABLES ON PAGES 56 TO 59, TURN TO THE
RELEVANT PAGES AND TAKE A STEP
FORWARD IN YOUR OWN SELF-KNOWLEDGE.

THE MOON IN
ARIES

JUST AS CANCER IS THE FIRST WATER SIGN, SO ARIES IS THE FIRST
FIRE SIGN. BOTH SIGNS HAVE HIGH EMOTIONAL LEVELS. YOUR
ARIEN MOON ADDS ENTHUSIASM TO YOUR CHARACTER, WHICH YOU
ARE LIKELY TO EXPRESS AT A MOMENT'S NOTICE.

You will be eager to surge ahead with projects and to accept challenges. Cancerians are noted for being both brave and protective, and these qualities are strongly emphasized in your personality.

Self-expression
In some respects a combination of fire and water elements is not an easy one. But your fire sign Moon works positively, in that you will be far less apprehensive, and less introverted, than some Cancerians.

You are one of the tougher types of Cancerian, and will be able to cope extremely well during demanding and strenuous periods. Perhaps your instinctively adventurous spirit will encourage you to be something of an explorer, with a penchant for visiting unusual places.

Cancerian moods, spiced with sudden emotional flare-ups, could make you a force to be reckoned with.

You should try to control these impulsive outbursts; they might be more potent than you realize.

Romance
You are extremely passionate, and it is in your love life that your very high emotional level will be best expressed. However, whereas your Cancerian Sun makes you somewhat clinging, your Arien Moon dictates that you need an element of independence and freedom.

Your well-being
The Arien body area is the head: if you are worried, you may tend to get unpleasant headaches. These may also be due to slight kidney upsets.

Planning ahead
As well as having plenty of Cancerian shrewdness and a good business sense, you react extremely well to enterprising schemes and suggestions.

The Moon in Aries

You should, however, always think carefully before becoming over-involved in them, in order to avoid disappointment later.

Parenthood

A great sense of fun and a marked sentimental streak, colour your attitude to life – this will certainly rub off on your loved ones. Like all Cancerians, you will be keen to have children, but you will be less prone to worry about them than most people of your Sun sign. But make sure that you recognize the fact that, in due course, they will want to move away from home and live their own lives. Your Arien Moon should help you to understand this, and to ensure that you do not feel life is too empty once they have gone. Try to always be forward-looking, and to see life through your children's eyes; otherwise, your Cancerian nostalgia and sentimentality could create a generation gap.

THE MOON IN
TAURUS

AS AN EARTH SIGN, YOUR TAUREAN MOON WILL STABILIZE YOUR
CANCERIAN QUALITIES AND ADD A PRACTICAL INSTINCT,
AS WELL AS AN APTITUDE FOR MAKING MONEY. BEWARE OF
ACTING TOO POSSESSIVELY TOWARDS LOVED ONES.

Earth and water signs complement each other well and, while the Moon, which rules Cancer, exerts a very powerful influence over all Cancerians it is, by tradition, well placed in Taurus. As a result you will share many of the qualities commonly attributed to Taurus.

Self-expression
It is extremely important for you to feel both materially and emotionally secure. Provided you can do this, you will flourish and be able to express many positive and fine qualities.

Through Taurus, you are warm and affectionate, and will not find it difficult to combine these traits with your caring, protective Cancerian ones. But you must ensure that possessiveness, which is the worst Taurean fault, does not obscure your warmth and kindness. On another level, your Cancerian instinct towards hoarding things, together with your

instinctive love of possessions, will very possibly make it difficult for you to throw anything away.

Romance
You have the capacity to love both deeply and very passionately. Cancerians are noted for the sensual expression of their emotions and, when this is combined with the warm passion of a Taurean Moon, your partners may consider themselves very fortunate indeed. You have the ability to make and maintain a long-lasting relationship.

Your well-being
The Taurean body area is the throat, so yours may well be vulnerable. More importantly, if you happen to be one of those marvellous Cancerian cooks, the likelihood is that you will specialize in making very rich desserts with lots of cream, chocolate, and liqueurs. Many Cancerians tend to

The Moon in Taurus

put on weight easily, and Taurean good looks are often endangered by their liking for good food. In short, be careful. If you have a slow metabolism, try to speed it up a little, perhaps through exercise.

Planning ahead

Cancerian shrewdness combines extremely well with the Taurean ability, for which you have a very natural instinct, to make money. There should be no problems when you have money to invest. In fact, if

you discuss your finances with professional advisers, you could end up advising them.

Parenthood

Given the Cancerian tendency to cling, and Taurean possessiveness, you should be constantly aware of the problems that can arise when you are bringing up children. Still, you have the potential to be a marvellous parent. You will be sensitive to your children's needs, giving them much love and affection.

THE MOON IN
GEMINI

WITH VERY LITTLE EFFORT, YOU PROBABLY COME UP WITH
PERTINENT AND WITTY RESPONSES. GEMINIAN LOGIC
COMES IN HANDY WHEN YOUR CANCERIAN IMAGINATION OR
WORRY GET THE BETTER OF YOU.

The elements – Cancer is a water sign and Gemini, air – add a variety of interesting facets to your personality. You are quick to respond to situations, and are able to act rationally when under stress. Your Cancerian tendency to worry will probably be filtered by an ability to look at problems very objectively.

A powerful Cancerian trait is moodiness. Here, however, your Geminian Moon helps to steady you; it will influence your reactions, and create a balance.

Self-expression

Cancerians usually have very powerful imaginations, but sometimes this potential is not quite as well developed as it should be. Your Geminian Moon will help, since it will intellectualize this area. You may have an ability for story-telling or writing, or for using your hands creatively in craftwork of all kinds. Geminians can

be rather restless and inconsistent. Always make sure that you go on to complete every project that you begin, and counter any restlessness and inconsistency.

Romance

You may not be quite as easily overwhelmed by emotion as many people of your Sun sign. Like all of them, however, you are a marvellously caring and protective lover.

It is also very important for you to have a good tie of friendship within your relationship, and to share common interests with your partner. You should consider this very carefully before deciding to deepen an emotional relationship.

Your well-being

The Geminian body area covers the arms and hands; if you are a Cancerian cook or work with metals or tools, these may be especially vulnerable.

The Moon in Gemini

The Geminian organ is the lungs. If you get a cold that settles on your chest, you should seek medical advice as soon as possible.

Planning ahead
Although you will probably possess Cancerian shrewdness and instinctively sound business sense, you may be attracted to get-rich-quick schemes. If this is the case, be wary of your initial reactions, as they could let you down. Always take your time when making decisions of this kind.

You may well have the ability to sell, and are likely to get a good price for anything you want to dispose of. Cancerians are natural collectors and you may be attracted to gadgets of some kind, such as animated toys.

Parenthood
You are more modern in outlook, more logical, and far less clinging than most other Cancerian parents. Being less sentimental and nostalgic than many Cancerians, the generation gap should not be a problem for you.

THE MOON IN
CANCER

WITH BOTH THE SUN AND THE MOON IN CANCER ON THE DAY
OF YOUR BIRTH, YOU WERE BORN UNDER A NEW MOON, AND
ARE KNOWN AS A DOUBLE CANCER. SINCE THE MOON RULES
CANCER, YOU MAY BE VERY CANCERIAN INDEED.

Reading a list of the attributes of your sensitive, caring Sun sign, you will probably recognize that a great many of them apply to you. On average, out of a list of 20 personality traits of any particular Sun sign, most people will identify with 11 or 12. Because the Moon was also in Cancer when you were born, for you the average increases considerably.

Self-expression

Your Sun sign makes you caring; you will like to cherish and look after people. Your Moon sign makes this even more your chief motivation. You will tend to be both moody and changeable, and it is very necessary that you recognize these tendencies.

It is also important for you to realize that, like the crab which is the symbol of your sign, you can easily become rather "snappy", expressing your feelings in a remarkably terse, sharp, and hurtful way.

You should find some way of positively expressing your powerful emotions. It is an excellent idea for you to have at least one compelling interest aside from your career or home and family.

Romance

You have a great deal of love to give to your partner; this is probably the most important area of emotional expression for you. But it may well be that your imagination will need to find expression. It can make you a stunning lover, capable of giving great pleasure to your partners, but it could mean that you will always be worried about them. You may find yourself either becoming jealous or thinking that the worst has happened to them.

Your well-being

As far as your health is concerned, if you read pages 22 to 23 you will probably agree that you suffer from

The Moon in Cancer

most Cancerian ailments. Many of these relate to the tendencies to worry that have been described here.

Planning ahead

You will often read that Cancerians are very shrewd in business. Because both your Sun sign and your Moon sign are in Cancer, you rightly conclude that you would be wise to follow your instincts in this area.

Even more than many people, you like to feel the security of a healthy bank balance, although Cancerians sometimes tend to be a little tight-fisted when it comes to actually spending their money. You probably know that Cancerians are the collectors (and also the hoarders!) of the Zodiac. Any unusual articles that you care to collect may well become valuable assets in the long term.

Parenthood

You will be keen to have children, and should make an excellent parent. Recognize that your children are individuals, who will want to create their own lifestyles and eventually start families. If you avoid being sentimental and nostalgic, the generation gap will not be a problem.

THE MOON IN
LEO

CANCER AND LEO ARE NEIGHBOURING ZODIAC SIGNS, AND OFFER
THEIR SUBJECTS VERY CONTRASTING CHARACTERISTICS. IF YOU
HAVE AN INSTINCTIVE URGE TO BE CREATIVE, DO NOT LET ANYONE,
INCLUDING YOURSELF, CRAMP YOUR STYLE.

Your natural Cancerian caution contrasts vividly with the nature of your Leo Moon, which is a fire sign. You will therefore respond to most things with greater enthusiasm than many Sun sign Cancerians. You will also be less apprehensive and much better organized.

Self-expression

The Cancerian tendency towards untidiness will be considerably mitigated by your Leo Moon; it gives you a certain style and elegance that many Cancerians tend to lack. Leo creativity blends well with the Cancerian instinct for imaginative design, and finding some form of creative expression could be of great importance to you.

The worst Leo fault is bossiness. If you are accused of this, take heed. You respond extremely quickly to other people's remarks and actions and, when this trait is combined with

the Cancerian tendency to be critically aggressive, you will see how, for you, sparks might occasionally fly.

Romance

Your Leo Moon gives you very warm and passionate emotions that will be beautifully expressed towards your loved ones. Sexually, you are probably quite assertive, and perhaps more keen to take the lead than many other Sun sign Cancerians.

Because Cancerians are sensitive, you could easily be hurt if difficulties arise within a relationship. In spite of the fact that your Leo Moon makes you brave and assertive in this area, when hurt you will creep into your Cancerian shell and lick your wounds.

Your well-being

The Leo body area is the spine, and you really need to indulge in a little exercise to keep it in good condition. If you have a sedentary job, make

The Moon in Leo

quite sure that you have a backrest chair, or at least one that properly supports your spine.

The Leo organ is the heart: if you follow the suggestions for exercising your spine, you will automatically be strengthening your heart, too.

Planning ahead
It is very likely that, although you have a shrewd Cancerian business sense, you will enjoy luxury and real quality more than many people of your Sun sign. In order to keep your Cancerian conscience happy, it might be wise to consider quality when you go shopping – that way you will get value for money and thoroughly enjoy what you may consider to be slightly extravagant. Do not be afraid to think big where investment is concerned.

Parenthood
You will be a very lively, positive, and encouraging parent. If you keep the negative side of your imagination under control, you will not worry unduly about your children. Try to avoid any stubborn or dogmatic reactions to their ideas and suggestions, and you will also avoid the development of a generation gap.

THE MOON IN
VIRGO

CANCER AND VIRGO ARE THE TWO ZODIAC SIGNS MOST PRONE TO
WORRY. CANCERIAN WORRY IS INTUITIVE AND IMAGINATIVE;
VIRGOAN, MORE INTELLECTUALLY ORIENTED. TRY TO BALANCE
ONE WITH THE OTHER.

Water and earth are considered to be complementary elements. Therefore since Cancer is a sign of the water element, and Virgo a sign of the earth element, the influences of your Sun and Moon signs generally work well together.

Self-expression
Cancer and Virgo certainly share some positive common attributes, but the signs also vie with each other to be the worst worriers of the Zodiac. Cancerian worry is emotional; Virgoan worry is illogical. But Cancerians are cautious, and Virgoans are practical. These traits will help to counter the difficulty. Try to be more logical, and bolster this with Cancerian caution.

Romance
Your Cancerian emotions may be slightly inhibited when you need to express your feelings towards lovers. Virgoans are very modest and, when

someone declares their affection for you, your immediate reaction may well be to recoil a little. Try to recognize the tendency, as it could limit your marvellously sensitive, sensual, and caring qualities.

You will tend to be very critical of your partners, and may nag them. If you are accused of this, take heed.

Your well-being
The Virgoan body area is the stomach; your digestive system is related to your Cancerian Sun. Worrying can therefore upset your stomach. Virgoans are also prone to nervous tension and stress, which can lead to migraine. Try to develop a sense of inner calm – a relaxation technique like yoga will be of help.

Planning ahead
Your Cancerian Sun sign makes you careful with money; your Virgoan Moon sign makes you even more

The Moon in Virgo

cautious. You therefore have the ability to save wisely. Just be sure to remember to enjoy the fruits of your labours. When investing, look for slow, steady growth.

Parenthood

Although Cancerians generally make warm, caring, and protective parents, you may tend to criticize your children a little too easily. This can be far more damaging than you might realize, especially if you have lively,

exuberant children. If you over-criticize them, they will probably lose their self-confidence. In the long term, this could obviously lead to problems, so guard against it.

Your creative imagination will stand you in good stead with your children. You are less likely than most people to have difficulty with the generation gap, since you will keep a keen and alert eye on the values and opinions of the younger generation, and will often provoke discussions.

THE MOON IN
LIBRA

IF YOUR INSTINCT TELLS YOU TO SWITCH OFF, CALM DOWN
AND RELAX. BY FOLLOWING IT, YOU WILL MAKE THE
MOST OF YOUR FINE, DIPLOMATIC MOON IN LIBRA, AND KEEP
YOURSELF IN BALANCE.

Both Cancer and Libra share the cardinal quality, and this makes for some interesting personality traits among those with this combination.

Self-expression
No matter how busy you may be, the chances are that you will always have time for others. As a result, you may well give the impression that you spend most of your time simply lazing about. That is not, of course, the case. You will work hard to achieve whatever you set out to do.

You are diplomatic, and probably less likely than most Cancerians to give way to moodiness. You also have a natural instinct for beautiful things, and will like your environment and personal appearance to be pleasing.

Romance
A natural indecisiveness may make committing yourself rather more difficult for you than for many people.

Once that commitment has been made, however, your Cancerian need for home and family life will be satisfied, and you will become a wonderful partner.

You have a strong inclination towards romance, and this does a great deal to enhance your love and sex life. There is an air of calm and serenity about you – but this will not inhibit passionate Cancerian emotion.

Your well-being
The Libran organ is the kidneys. Recurrent headaches could indicate that you have a minor kidney disorder. On the other hand, headaches could be the result of the Cancerian tendency to worry. Your Libran Moon will work very much in your favour in this area, telling you to calm down, switch off, and relax.

Bearing in mind that you could well love gourmet cooking and delicious food, and remembering that Librans

The Moon in Libra

often have a sweet tooth, there is obviously a danger that you may put on weight easily. Try to take regular workouts at a large and friendly health club where there is the possibility of socializing after class.

Planning ahead

Cancerian financial caution could dampen a marvellously luxurious, pleasure-loving instinct given you by your Libran Moon. Look at it in this way: you are clever with money, and have no lack of shrewdness, so why

not give in to your love of luxury? It will make life fun, far more enjoyable, and will certainly help you to relax.

Parenthood

You will probably have a more relaxed attitude to parenthood than many other Sun sign Cancerians, but should be very careful that you do not confuse your children by being indecisive. You will always be happy to listen to your children, so in that respect there should be no difficulty with the generation gap.

THE MOON IN
SCORPIO

CANCER AND SCORPIO ARE BOTH SIGNS OF THE WATER ELEMENT.
YOUR MOON GIVES YOU A TERRIFIC SOURCE OF EMOTIONAL
ENERGY; CHANNEL THIS WISELY, AND DO NOT RESORT TO BEING
JEALOUS OR VINDICTIVE.

Because both Cancer and Scorpio are water signs, you are likely to have tremendous resources of emotional and physical energy. You must find fulfilling ways of expressing these, because inner satisfaction and psychological wholeness are of above-average importance to you.

Self-expression
Your work must satisfy you. If its demands are not enough for you and your lifestyle is equally unengaging, then develop a compelling spare-time interest. This should consume either your emotional or physical energy; or ideally, both. Cancerian tenacity and your urge to get to the bottom of every problem will blend well, whatever you do.

Romance
You have a great deal to contribute to a long-term relationship. As an extremely passionate lover, you can,

however, be very demanding both sexually and in more general matters. You need an understanding partner, who will be as keen as you are to live an active and full life. Should any Cancerian moods catch up with you, your partner will need to be considerate enough to understand.

The worst Scorpio fault is jealousy. If you allow your Cancerian imagination to work overtime you really could build up the most awful tension in a relationship. Try to accept rational explanations and recognize that logic can escape you.

Your well-being
The Scorpio body area is the genitals, so regular health checks of this area are most advisable. You could be more prone to worry than is usual for Cancerians, and this could also have an effect upon your health. Remember, too, that a boring job will leave you lacking inner satisfaction.

The Moon in Scorpio

Planning ahead

You may have a really good business sense, and perhaps a desire to set up and develop your own company. You are shrewd; your Cancerian Sun sees to that. But your Scorpio Moon will also stand you in excellent stead here.

Parenthood

Your Cancerian Sun makes you a good, but demanding, parent – it could be that you are considerably stricter than you may realize. You will be eager to spur your children into action, but be careful not to be too dogmatic. Encourage them, but remember that finding the appropriate kind of encouragement for each child may be difficult. Try not to be too keen for your children to follow in your footsteps; they may find their own paths more rewarding. If you allow them the freedom of expression that is so necessary to young people, you will avoid problems with the generation gap.

THE MOON IN
SAGITTARIUS

YOUR SAGITTARIAN INSTINCT IS FOR FREEDOM OF EXPRESSION
AND INDEPENDENCE, BUT YOU ALSO VALUE CANCERIAN
EMOTIONAL SECURITY AND YOUR FAMILY. LEARN TO COMPROMISE,
WHILE RETAINING YOUR OWN SPACE.

The combination of a Cancerian Sun and a Sagittarian Moon gives your personality some contrasting and very unusual aspects. It may even be that when you read descriptions of your Sun sign, you think some of the statements hold little or no truth at all.

Self-expression

You are likely to have a wider-ranging mind than other Sun sign Cancerians, incorporating qualities that differ from those normally associated with your Sun sign. While, for instance, you love and need the security of your home and family, claustrophobic feelings – brought on either by the physical layout of your home, or more psychologically because of an over-commitment to your family – are something that you really cannot cope with. It is important that you respond freely to the outgoing, extrovert levels of your personality. Do not let

Cancerian sensitivity or inhibition cramp the open expression of your Moon sign qualities.

Romance

Your attitude towards love is very positive. You will like to have fun and enjoy your relationships. Sagittarius is a very emotional sign, and you therefore have abundant quantities of outgoing emotion and passion.

It may be that you will take rather longer than many people of your Sun sign to settle into a permanent relationship. Before you do so, remember that you really need an intelligent partner, who will be prepared to stretch your mind.

Your well-being

The Sagittarian body area covers the hips and thighs. If you are a female Cancerian cook or simply love good food, you will tend to put on weight very easily around these areas. Male

The Moon in Sagittarius

Cancerians can all too easily develop heavy stomachs. Fortunately, you probably love sport and are keen to participate in it. If this is not the case, try some kind of freely expressive dance. In complete contrast, horse-riding may appeal to you.

Planning ahead

A tendency to take risks can make you a little foolhardy when dealing with money. Remember, however, that Cancerians are usually shrewd and clever both in business and when dealing with cash. Try, therefore, to get the best of both your Sun sign and

your Moon sign, and learn to enjoy the challenge of making money grow without letting a deep-rooted gambling instinct overpower you.

Parenthood

You will have a very positive attitude towards your children and, unlike many Cancerians, will probably not worry if they are a few minutes late home from school. You can inspire them and, if you allow an instinctive and very natural sense of enthusiasm full rein, you will gain their love and respect. You should have few problems with the generation gap.

THE MOON IN
CAPRICORN

CANCER AND CAPRICORN ARE OPPOSITE OR POLAR ZODIAC SIGNS,
SO YOU WERE BORN UNDER A FULL MOON. YOU ARE
INHERENTLY PRONE TO RESTLESSNESS AND AN INNER DISCONTENT;
TRY TO COUNTER ANY TENDENCY TO GRUMBLE.

You will probably be rather more ambitious, and aspire to greater achievements, than other Sun sign Cancerians. But because Capricorn is not particularly emotionally oriented, it may be that this ambition, which is usually so strong, will remain subdued. It is important that you do not suppress it.

Self-expression

Both Cancer and Capricorn are of the cardinal quality and, as a result, you possess the ability to use your energies freely and willingly for the benefit of others. In regard to yourself, you really do have an instinct that could lead you to the top of your own individual "mountain".

Be careful of one thing: you may have a tendency to grumble, especially when presented with challenges or suggestions that do not precisely fit in with your plans. This will not make you popular with other people. Be aware, too, that because you were born under a Full Moon you could tend to suffer from restlessness.

Romance

While Cancerian warmth and tenderness will colour your attitude towards your partners, your first reaction when approached by a prospective lover could be slightly cool. They may well have to break down that chilliness, and indeed the self-defensive Cancerian protective shell that could very easily manifest itself should you begin to feel in the least vulnerable or insecure. But your lover, having gained your confidence, really does have someone very special; you are more than likely to remain faithful forever.

Your well-being

The Capricornian body areas are the shins and knees. These, and your joints in general, are rather prone to

The Moon in Capricorn

stiffness and rheumatic pain. It is vital for you to find a form of exercise that will help you to keep mobile.

Planning ahead

One way in which the Cancerian and Capricornian "polarity" emerges is through the fact that both signs are known to be very careful with money. A little more generosity may create a more enjoyable lifestyle for you.

Your Capricornian Moon gives you a natural inclination and instinct for real quality. You like to buy things that will really last – partly because you hate waste and probably loathe throwing things away. You will invest very wisely and, in general, will always aim for steady growth.

Parenthood

Avoid the tendency to distance yourself from your children. Make sure that you have fun, and that the quirky sense of humour which comes from your Capricornian Moon finds plenty of expression. By doing so, you will bridge the generation gap.

THE MOON IN
AQUARIUS

TRY NOT TO BE AFRAID OF EXPRESSING YOUR UNCONVENTIONAL
ORIGINALITY: IT OFFERS YOU THE CHANCE TO FIND
CONSIDERABLE INNER SATISFACTION AND FULFILMENT. DO NOT
INSTINCTIVELY DISTANCE YOURSELF FROM OTHERS.

Your air sign Aquarian Moon and water sign Cancerian Sun are not the easiest of bedfellows. You will, however, have some extremely interesting and unusual qualities that make you a truly fascinating person.

Self-expression

Your reactions to situations are somewhat unpredictable. On some occasions you can be sympathetic, but on others, shocked. Your Cancerian kindness and sensitivity are, however, marvellously enhanced by some very humanitarian qualities. You will give both time and energy, as well as money, when and where you come across need – it will be this sense of need that instinctively motivates you. Having taken action, you will freely express your caring, protective Cancerian spirit.

Your Cancerian emotions are somewhat cooled by your Moon sign influences. You are able to rationalize your feelings and, if it becomes necessary, should be able to distance yourself from them.

Romance

At heart, you are very romantic, but it could be that an inner need for independence clashes with a desire to have your own home and family. You may be attracted to a lifestyle that is individual in some way.

A love of romance is never too far from the surface and, because of it, you are likely to enjoy love and sex in a romantic atmosphere. It should not be difficult for you to persuade your partner to go along with this. Since you have an intriguing air of glamour, and are attractive to the opposite sex, you should enjoy yourself.

Your well-being

The Aquarian body area is the ankles, and these are very vulnerable. The circulation is also governed by

The Moon in Aquarius

Aquarius, so you really do need to take care of yourself when the weather is cold.

Planning ahead
Of all the Cancerian Sun and Moon sign combinations, yours may be the least practical when it comes to money. Of course, you have Cancerian shrewdness and business sense lurking somewhere in your personality. You could actually be a lot cleverer than you realize in these matters, and may be wasting your potential. If you see yourself owning a business, bear in mind that you stand a good chance of succeeding.

Parenthood
As a parent, your tendency to be unpredictable, plus Cancerian changes of mood, may cause difficulties. Keeping abreast of your children's ideas and concerns will help you to come to terms with any generation gap problems.

THE MOON IN
PISCES

A TENDER AND LOVING CANCERIAN, WITH THE POWERFUL,
EMOTIONALLY ORIENTATED FORCE OF PISCES, HAS A
TORRENT OF EMOTIONAL ENERGY. USE THAT ENERGY, AND NEVER
UNDERESTIMATE YOURSELF AND YOUR ABILITIES.

While the combination of two water signs will serve to integrate your instincts and self-expression successfully, you should be careful that you are not entirely swayed by your reactions to people, and by the power of your emotions.

Self-expression
You will automatically follow your intuition and natural instincts. Remember, though, that because you are so very kind, helpful, and charitable, and always ready to part with time, energy, and cash, people could all too easily take advantage of you. You may consciously have to develop your protective Cancerian shell at times and, if you wish to have complete control over your life, you will have to be firm with yourself.

Your Cancerian Sun gives you inner strength and tenacity, but a very tender and ultra-sensitive Piscean Moon could sometimes tend to undermine your more powerful characteristics, especially when you are moved in some way.

Romance
If you get caught up with a partner who does not allow you the freedom to develop your potential and use your vivid imagination, think again.

You need a strong partner who will encourage you in all your efforts and take some of the strain, should an area of your life fall under pressure. There is a romantic, almost poetic, side to you, which colours your expression of love and sex – your partners really should enjoy it. Be careful that you do not delude yourself when you are in love, seeing every partner as your ideal, and try not to be deceptive.

Your well-being
The Piscean body area is the feet. These could cause you a lot of trouble. On the other hand, as can be

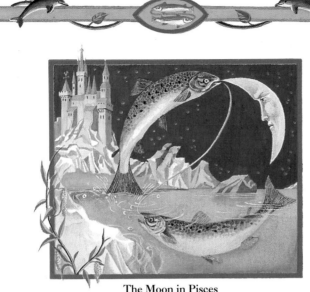

The Moon in Pisces

the case with astrology, quite the reverse could be true, and your feet may be healthy and problem-free.

The Cancerian tendency to worry will certainly affect you. Make sure that this does not become irrational, and that your very powerful imagination does not take over. Be guided by your intuition, and control any exaggerated reactions.

Planning ahead
Your Piscean Moon may overcome your practical, cautious Cancerian qualities when it comes to dealing with money. If you are aware of this,

then perhaps, over a period of time, you will learn not to be a financial soft touch. Take advice from your bank manager, accountant, or from some other professional.

Parenthood
Children are very artful and, from an early age, could learn how to get around you. It may be necessary for you to act strictly from time to time.

Try not to be too clinging and sentimental, and remember that if you do not keep up with your children's way of thinking, you may have generation gap problems.

MOON CHARTS

REFER TO THE FOLLOWING TABLES TO DISCOVER YOUR MOON SIGN.
THE PRECEDING PAGES WILL TELL YOU ABOUT ITS QUALITIES.

By referring to the Moon charts opposite and overleaf, look up the year of your birth and the Zodiacal glyph for your birth month. Refer next to the Moon Table (*below, left*) in which the days of the month are listed against a number. The number against the day of the month in which you were born indicates how many Zodiacal glyphs (*below, right*) must be counted before you reach your Moon sign. You may have to count to Pisces and return to Aries. For example, given the birthdate 21 May 1991, you initially need to find the Moon sign

for the first day of May in that year. It is Sagittarius (♐). With the birthdate falling on the 21st, nine signs must be added. The Moon sign for this birth date is therefore Virgo (♍).

Note that because the Moon moves so quickly, it is beyond the scope of this little book to provide a detailed chart of its positions. For more detailed horoscopes, consult an astrologer, but if you feel that this chart gives a result that does not seem to apply to you, read the pages for the signs either before or after the one indicated; one of the three will apply.

MOON TABLE

DAYS OF THE MONTH AND NUMBER OF SIGNS THAT SHOULD BE ADDED

DAY	ADD	DAY	ADD	DAY	ADD	DAY	ADD
1	0	9	4	17	7	25	11
2	1	10	4	18	8	26	11
3	1	11	5	19	8	27	12
4	1	12	5	20	9	28	12
5	2	13	5	21	9	29	1
6	2	14	6	22	10	30	1
7	3	15	6	23	10	31	2
8	3	16	7	24	10		

ZODIACAL GLYPHS

♈	Aries
♉	Taurus
♊	Gemini
♋	Cancer
♌	Leo
♍	Virgo
♎	Libra
♏	Scorpio
♐	Sagittarius
♑	Capricorn
♒	Aquarius
♓	Pisces

	1923	1924	1925	1926	1927	1928	1929	1930	1931	1932	1933	1934	1935
JAN	♊	♏	♈	♌	♐	♈	♍	♑	♉	♎	♓	♋	♏
FEB	♌	♐	♉	♍	♑	♊	♏	♓	♋	♐	♈	♌	♑
MAR	♌	♑	♉	♍	♒	♋	♏	♓	♋	♐	♉	♍	♑
APR	♎	♓	♋	♏	♈	♍	♑	♉	♍	♒	♊	♎	♓
MAY	♏	♈	♌	♐	♉	♎	♒	♊	♎	♓	♋	♐	♈
JUN	♑	♉	♍	♒	♋	♏	♓	♌	♐	♍	♑	♊	♊
JUL	♒	♋	♏	♓	♌	♐	♈	♍	♑	♊	♎	♓	♋
AUG	♈	♌	♐	♉	♍	♒	♊	♏	♓	♋	♐	♈	♌
SEP	♉	♎	♒	♋	♏	♓	♌	♐	♈	♍	♑	♊	♎
OCT	♊	♏	♓	♌	♐	♉	♍	♑	♉	♎	♓	♋	♏
NOV	♌	♑	♉	♍	♑	♊	♏	♓	♋	♐	♈	♌	♑
DEC	♍	♒	♊	♎	♓	♌	♐	♈	♌	♑	♉	♍	♒

	1936	1937	1938	1939	1940	1941	1942	1943	1944	1945	1946	1947	1948
JAN	♈	♌	♑	♉	♍	♒	♊	♎	♓	♌	♐	♈	♍
FEB	♉	♎	♒	♊	♏	♈	♌	♐	♉	♍	♑	♊	♎
MAR	♊	♎	♒	♋	♐	♈	♌	♐	♉	♎	♒	♊	♏
APR	♌	♐	♈	♌	♑	♉	♎	♒	♋	♏	♓	♌	♑
MAY	♍	♑	♉	♎	♒	♊	♏	♓	♌	♐	♉	♍	♒
JUN	♎	♒	♋	♏	♈	♌	♑	♉	♎	♒	♊	♏	♓
JUL	♏	♈	♌	♑	♉	♍	♒	♊	♏	♓	♌	♐	♈
AUG	♑	♉	♎	♒	♋	♏	♈	♌	♐	♉	♍	♑	♊
SEP	♓	♋	♏	♈	♌	♑	♉	♍	♒	♋	♏	♓	♌
OCT	♈	♌	♑	♉	♎	♒	♊	♎	♓	♌	♐	♈	♍
NOV	♊	♎	♒	♊	♏	♈	♌	♐	♉	♍	♑	♊	♏
DEC	♋	♏	♓	♌	♑	♉	♍	♑	♊	♎	♒	♋	♐

57

	1949	1950	1951	1952	1953	1954	1955	1956	1957	1958	1959	1960	1961
JAN	♑	♊	♎	♓	♋	♏	♈	♌	♑	♉	♍	♒	♋
FEB	♓	♋	♐	♈	♍	♑	♉	♎	♒	♊	♏	♈	♌
MAR	♓	♋	♐	♉	♍	♑	♊	♏	♓	♋	♏	♈	♌
APR	♉	♏	♒	♊	♎	♓	♋	♐	♈	♌	♑	♊	♎
MAY	♊	♎	♓	♋	♐	♈	♍	♑	♉	♎	♒	♋	♏
JUN	♌	♐	♈	♍	♑	♊	♎	♓	♋	♐	♈	♌	♑
JUL	♍	♑	♊	♎	♓	♋	♏	♈	♌	♑	♉	♍	♒
AUG	♏	♓	♋	♐	♈	♍	♑	♉	♎	♒	♊	♏	♈
SEP	♐	♈	♍	♑	♊	♎	♒	♋	♐	♈	♌	♑	♊
OCT	♑	♊	♎	♓	♋	♏	♓	♌	♑	♉	♍	♒	♋
NOV	♓	♋	♏	♈	♍	♑	♉	♎	♒	♊	♏	♈	♌
DEC	♈	♌	♑	♊	♎	♒	♊	♏	♓	♌	♐	♉	♍

	1962	1963	1964	1965	1966	1967	1968	1969	1970	1971	1972	1973	1974
JAN	♏	♓	♌	♐	♈	♍	♑	♊	♎	♒	♋	♐	♈
FEB	♐	♉	♍	♒	♊	♏	♓	♋	♏	♈	♍	♑	♉
MAR	♐	♉	♎	♒	♊	♏	♈	♌	♐	♉	♍	♑	♉
APR	♒	♋	♏	♈	♌	♑	♉	♍	♒	♊	♏	♓	♋
MAY	♓	♌	♐	♉	♍	♒	♊	♎	♓	♋	♐	♈	♍
JUN	♉	♎	♒	♊	♏	♓	♌	♐	♉	♍	♑	♊	♎
JUL	♊	♏	♓	♌	♐	♈	♍	♑	♊	♎	♓	♋	♐
AUG	♌	♐	♉	♎	♒	♊	♍	♏	♋	♏	♈	♍	♑
SEP	♍	♒	♋	♏	♓	♋	♐	♉	♍	♑	♊	♎	♓
OCT	♏	♓	♌	♐	♈	♍	♒	♊	♎	♒	♋	♐	♈
NOV	♐	♉	♎	♒	♊	♎	♓	♋	♐	♈	♍	♑	♉
DEC	♑	♊	♏	♓	♋	♐	♈	♌	♑	♉	♎	♒	♊

	1975	1976	1977	1978	1979	1980	1981	1982	1983	1984	1985	1986	1987
JAN	♌	♑	♉	♍	♒	♊	♏	♓	♌	♐	♉	♍	♑
FEB	♎	♒	♋	♏	♈	♌	♐	♉	♍	♒	♊	♎	♓
MAR	♎	♓	♋	♏	♈	♍	♑	♉	♎	♒	♊	♏	♓
APR	♐	♈	♍	♑	♊	♎	♒	♋	♏	♈	♌	♑	♉
MAY	♑	♉	♎	♒	♋	♏	♓	♌	♐	♉	♍	♒	♊
JUN	♓	♋	♐	♈	♌	♑	♉	♎	♒	♊	♏	♓	♌
JUL	♈	♌	♑	♉	♍	♒	♋	♏	♓	♌	♐	♉	♍
AUG	♉	♎	♓	♋	♏	♈	♌	♐	♈	♎	♒	♊	♎
SEP	♋	♐	♈	♌	♐	♊	♎	♒	♊	♏	♓	♌	♐
OCT	♌	♑	♉	♍	♒	♋	♏	♓	♋	♐	♉	♍	♑
NOV	♎	♓	♋	♏	♓	♌	♐	♉	♍	♒	♊	♎	♓
DEC	♏	♈	♌	♐	♉	♍	♑	♊	♎	♓	♋	♐	♍

	1988	1989	1990	1991	1992	1993	1994	1995	1996	1997	1998	1999	2000
JAN	♊	♎	♒	♋	♏	♈	♌	♑	♉	♎	♒	♊	♏
FEB	♋	♐	♈	♍	♑	♉	♎	♒	♋	♏	♈	♌	♐
MAR	♌	♐	♉	♍	♒	♊	♎	♓	♋	♏	♈	♌	♑
APR	♍	♒	♊	♏	♓	♋	♐	♈	♍	♑	♊	♎	♓
MAY	♏	♓	♌	♐	♈	♍	♑	♉	♎	♒	♋	♏	♈
JUN	♐	♉	♍	♑	♊	♎	♓	♋	♐	♈	♌	♑	♉
JUL	♑	♊	♎	♒	♋	♐	♈	♌	♑	♉	♎	♒	♋
AUG	♓	♌	♐	♈	♍	♑	♉	♎	♓	♋	♏	♓	♌
SEP	♉	♍	♑	♊	♏	♓	♋	♏	♈	♌	♑	♉	♎
OCT	♊	♎	♒	♋	♐	♈	♌	♑	♉	♎	♒	♊	♏
NOV	♌	♐	♈	♍	♑	♉	♎	♒	♋	♏	♈	♌	♑
DEC	♍	♑	♉	♎	♒	♋	♏	♈	♌	♐	♉	♍	♒

THE SOLAR SYSTEM

THE STARS, OTHER THAN THE SUN, PLAY NO PART IN THE SCIENCE
OF ASTROLOGY. ASTROLOGERS USE ONLY THE BODIES IN THE
SOLAR SYSTEM, EXCLUDING THE EARTH, TO CALCULATE HOW OUR
LIVES AND PERSONALITIES CHANGE.

Pluto
Pluto takes 246 years to travel around
the Sun. It affects our unconscious
instincts and urges, gives us strength
in difficulty, and perhaps emphasizes
any inherent cruel streak.

Neptune
Neptune stays in each sign for 14
years. At best it makes us sensitive
and imaginative; at worst it
encourages deceit and carelessness,
making us worry.

Uranus
Uranus's influence can make us
friendly, kind, eccentric, inventive,
and unpredictable.

Saturn
In ancient times, Saturn was the most
distant known planet. Its influence
can limit our ambition and make us
either overly cautious (but practical),
or reliable and self-disciplined.

SATURN

PLUTO

NEPTUNE

URANUS

Jupiter

Jupiter encourages expansion, optimism, generosity, and breadth of vision. It can, however, also make us wasteful, extravagant, and conceited.

Mars

Much associated with energy, anger, violence, selfishness, and a strong sex drive, Mars also encourages decisiveness and leadership.

JUPITER

The Moon

Although it is a satellite of the Earth, the Moon is known in astrology as a planet. It lies about 240,000 miles from the Earth and, astrologically, is second in importance to the Sun.

MERCURY

THE MOON

VENUS

EARTH

MARS

The Sun

The Sun, the only star used by astrologers, influences the way we present ourselves to the world – our image or personality; the "us" we show to other people.

Venus

The planet of love and partnership, Venus can emphasize all our best personal qualities. It may also encourage us to be lazy, impractical, and too dependent on other people.

Earth

Every planet contributes to the environment of the Solar System, and a person born on Venus would no doubt be influenced by our own planet in some way.

Mercury

The planet closest to the Sun affects our intellect. It can make us inquisitive, versatile, argumentative, perceptive, and clever, but maybe also inconsistent, cynical, and sarcastic.